Hide in the Cave!

By Sally Cowan

Clove and Pete are skunk kits.

These two cute kits doze on a pile of pine stems.

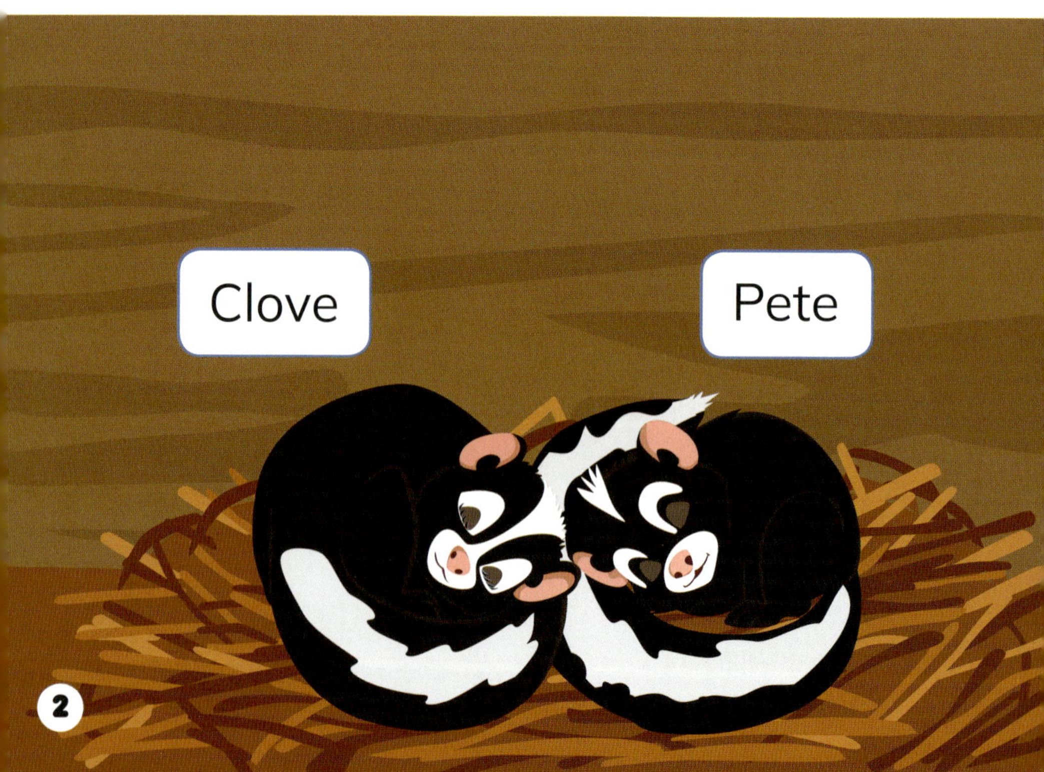

Wake up, kits!
It is time to hunt.

"What is the rule?" said Mum.

Then Mum froze.

She could see flames!

“We must hide!” said Mum.
“Let’s dive into this cave!”

A red truck came
with a big hose
to stop the blaze.

As the sun rises,

Pete pokes his nose up.

The skunks gaze
at the black trunks.

CHECKING FOR MEANING

1. Where are Clove and Pete at the start of the story? *(Literal)*
2. Where did the skunks hide from the blaze? *(Literal)*
3. Why did Mum say the kits were *quite brave*? *(Inferential)*

EXTENDING VOCABULARY

kits	In the story, the word *kits* refers to baby skunks. What else can *kit* mean?
doze	What are you doing if you doze? What other words do you know that mean the same thing?
gaze	What does it mean to gaze at something? What is another word that the author could have used instead of *gaze*?

MOVING BEYOND THE TEXT

1. What other names for baby animals do you know?
2. Skunks live in the forest. What other animals live in the forest?
3. The skunks went on a hunt for grubs. What other animals might eat grubs?
4. Why are firefighters an important part of our community?

TIME TO WRITE

Imagine you are Clove or Pete. Write about how you feel during the story.

PRACTICE WORDS